FAVORITE FOOD FRANCHISES

Chick-fil-A®

Laura Purdie Salas

Mitchell Lane
PUBLISHERS

Parent and Caregiver Tips for Creating Nonfiction Readers

The high-interest topics in the ***Favorite Food Franchises*** series are sure to get your young reader excited about reading nonfiction. While exploring a fascinating subject, your reader will be introduced to new facts, ideas, and vocabulary.

Tips for Reading Nonfiction

Talk about Nonfiction

Explain that nonfiction books provide facts about real-world topics. When readers read nonfiction, they gain a rich understanding of the world. They build background knowledge that provides a foundation for learning and academic success.

Look at the Parts

This book contains the following helpful features. Share the purpose of each feature with your reader.

Photos, Captions, and Graphic Aids
The photos, captions, maps, diagrams, time lines, and other graphic aids in nonfiction texts contain a wealth of information. Help your reader identify different ways information can be displayed.

Sidebars
These extra tidbits of information help satisfy readers' curiosity and expand their knowledge.

Table of Contents
Located at the front of the book, this list shows the big ideas within the text and the page numbers where they can be found.

Glossary
Located at the back of the book, the glossary defines key words and phrases that are related to the topic. These words and phrases can be found in the text in colored type.

Comprehension Questions (Fact Check)
Multiple-choice questions help readers self-check to make sure they understand what they read.

Index
Located at the back of the book, the index is an alphabetical list of topics and the page numbers where they can be found.

With a little help and guidance, your reader will be on their way to enjoying and learning from nonfiction books.

Mitchell Lane
PUBLISHERS

mitchelllanepub.com

2001 SW 31st Avenue
Hallandale, FL 33009

First Edition, 2025.
Author: Laura Purdie Salas
Designer: Rhea Magaro
Editor: Kim Thompson

Series: Favorite Food Franchises
Title: Chick-fil-a / by Laura Purdie Salas

Hallandale, FL : Mitchell Lane Publishers, [2025]

Library bound ISBN: 979-8-89260-310-2
Paperback ISBN: 979-8-89260-433-8
eBook ISBN: 979-8-89260-321-8

PHOTO CREDITS
Alamy: Allen Creative/Steve Allen, cover, 1, 10, 12, 13; Michael Neelon(misc), 3; ZUMA Press, Inc., 4, 24; Ken Hawkins, 9; Franck Fotos, 9; RSBPhoto, 14, 15; Ron Buskirk, 15; Keith Homan, 16; Stanley Leary, 27; B. David Cathell, 29; Shutterstock: MN Studios, cover, 1; dwph, cover; rangizzz, 6, 9, 13, 17, 19, 20, 24; Tim UR, 20, 21; aperturesound, 4; Kushal Bose, 7; James R. Martin, 7; AlenKadr, 13; ABBYDOG, 20; Gerry Matthews, 22; Jonathan Weiss, 22; DW labs Incorporated, 22; Triff, 22; Andriy Blokhin, 23; Greg finnegan, 23; P Maxwell Photography, 32; Rhea Magaro: 5; 17, 18, 19, 21; Library of Congress: 8; Chick-fil-a: 11

CONTENTS

THE CHICK-FIL-A WAY

The Chick-fil-A® chicken sandwich is more than 60 years old. It's true! **Founder** S. Truett Cathy perfected the recipe in 1964.

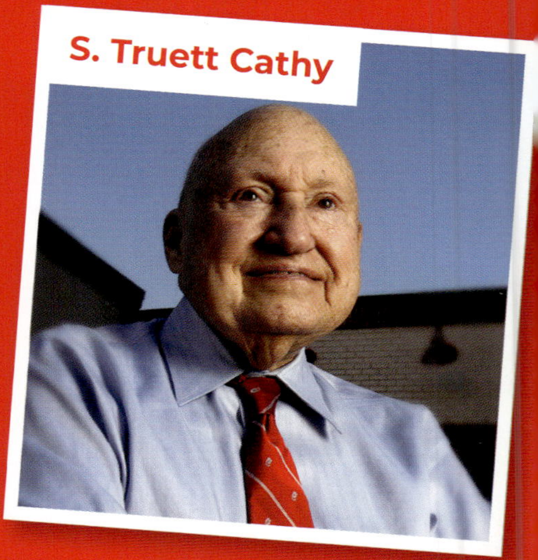

The recipe hasn't changed since then. The sandwich is still made with a breaded chicken breast. The chicken still goes on a buttered bun with two dill pickle chips.

The exact recipe is a secret. It's locked in a safe in Atlanta, Georgia.

Religion is important to Chick-fil-A. It's a Christian business. The company says that part of its purpose is to glorify God.

Chick-fil-A restaurants close on Sundays. Cathy decided this even before he opened his first restaurant. He wanted workers to be able to rest on Sundays and go to church with their families.

Quick Chick Fact

Not everyone agrees with Chick-fil-A's religious views. Some people say the company has given money to groups that support injustice.

Chick-fil-A
BREAKFAST
CLOSED SUNDAY

AN EMPIRE BEGINS

S. Truett Cathy was a Georgia boy. He grew up during the **Great Depression**. He learned to work hard at a young age.

Cathy served six years in the United States Army. Afterward, he wanted to open a restaurant. He and his brother Ben started the Dwarf Grill in 1946.

In 1967, Cathy opened a new restaurant. It was the very first Chick-fil-A. The menu starred his **pressure-cooked** chicken sandwich.

The Great Depression

The Dwarf Grill (later changed to Dwarf House) in Hapeville, GA

Quick Chick Fact

True to its name, the Dwarf Grill was tiny. Originally, it had only 10 stools and four tables.

TRUETT'S
Chick-fil-A

That first Chick-fil-A was in Atlanta's Greenbriar Shopping Center. Back in 1967, people just shopped at malls. They didn't eat there.

But the restaurant with only six chairs was a success. Shoppers lined up out into the mall to get their chicken sandwiches.

People enjoyed Chick-fil-A's food. And they liked having food close to where they shopped. That store was the start of the Chick-fil-A **empire**. It also inspired the invention of the food court.

PART OF THE SCENERY

Today, most Chick-fil-A **franchises** are in stand-alone buildings with bright lights and wooden tables. But not all locations look alike. You'll always spot the red and white logo, though. And you may see two cows—more on them later!

Some decorations honor Chick-fil-A's Georgia roots. For example, big wooden light shades resemble peach baskets. Georgia is famous for growing peaches.

One New York City location is very different. It's five stories tall. There's even rooftop dining!

Quick Chick Fact

Some Chick-fil-As have light fixtures made of glass Coca-Cola® bottles. The Coca-Cola company is based in Atlanta. Truett used to sell bottles of Coke for five cents.

Chick-fil-A restaurants are bustling places. Families crowd booths and tables. Kids play in the play space. Teens hang out at the **gathering table**. Workers at the counter take orders, fill drinks, and hand bags to delivery drivers.

Usually, cars flood the drive-thru. In busy times, workers stand outside with tablets to take orders face-to-face.

However you get your Chick-fil-A order, one thing's always the same. When you thank a Chick-fil-A worker, they will smile and say, "My pleasure." That's the response the company is known for.

CHICKEN CHOICES

Chick-fil-A is all about chicken. There's grilled chicken and fried chicken. There are chicken breasts and chicken nuggets. There are chicken sandwiches, salads, and wraps. If you want chicken, Chick-fil-A has you covered!

There are other options too. You can get fries or fruit. Soup or mac and cheese. Tea or lemonade. These additional menu items may be tasty, but they are mostly there just to **complement** the chicken.

Quick Chick Fact

In the early 1980s, some customers requested chicken sandwiches cut into tiny pieces that would be easy to serve at parties. In 1982, Chick-fil-A began selling chicken nuggets.

Chick-fil-A makes its **signature** chicken sandwich fresh. A worker dips a raw chicken breast into **marinade**. Then, they coat it in seasoned breading.

The worker puts many chicken breasts into a metal basket. Dividers in the basket keep the chicken from sticking together.

Next, the basket goes into a pressure cooker. The chicken fries in boiling peanut oil. The worker puts the chicken on a buttered, toasted bun with two pickles on it. The sandwich is ready to go.

Quick Chick Fact

Chick-fil-A's sauces are almost as famous as its chicken! Chick-fil-A Sauce is tangy, smoky, and a little bit mustardy. Other sauce choices are barbecue, buffalo, ranch, and sweet and sour.

Chick-fil-A was built on fried chicken. But it has healthier food too. Just step away from the fryer.

Chick-fil-A started grilling chicken in 1989. Over time, they've tested more than 1,200 seasoning combinations. They even have grilled chicken nuggets.

Quick Chick Fact

Chick-fil-A used **antibiotic-free** chicken for years. In 2024, they began using chickens treated with some antibiotics. Many people disagreed with this decision.

For a smart choice, try some grilled chicken. Add an applesauce. Wash it down with milk. There you go—a Chick-fil-A meal that is good for you!

FAR-FLUNG SUCCESS

In 1967, Chick-fil-A was one tiny restaurant in a mall. It spread to other malls during the 1970s and 1980s. Then, Chick-fil-A began building stand-alone restaurants.

Today, more than 3,000 Chick-fil-As dot the United States, Puerto Rico, and Canada. They're in airports and on college campuses. They're found in small towns, suburbs, and big cities.

The company is a huge success. Its sales topped 18 billion dollars in 2022 alone. S. Truett Cathy's family still owns 100 percent of the company.

Quick Chick Fact

Chick-fil-A sponsors the Peach Bowl. This college football game is played in Atlanta every year.

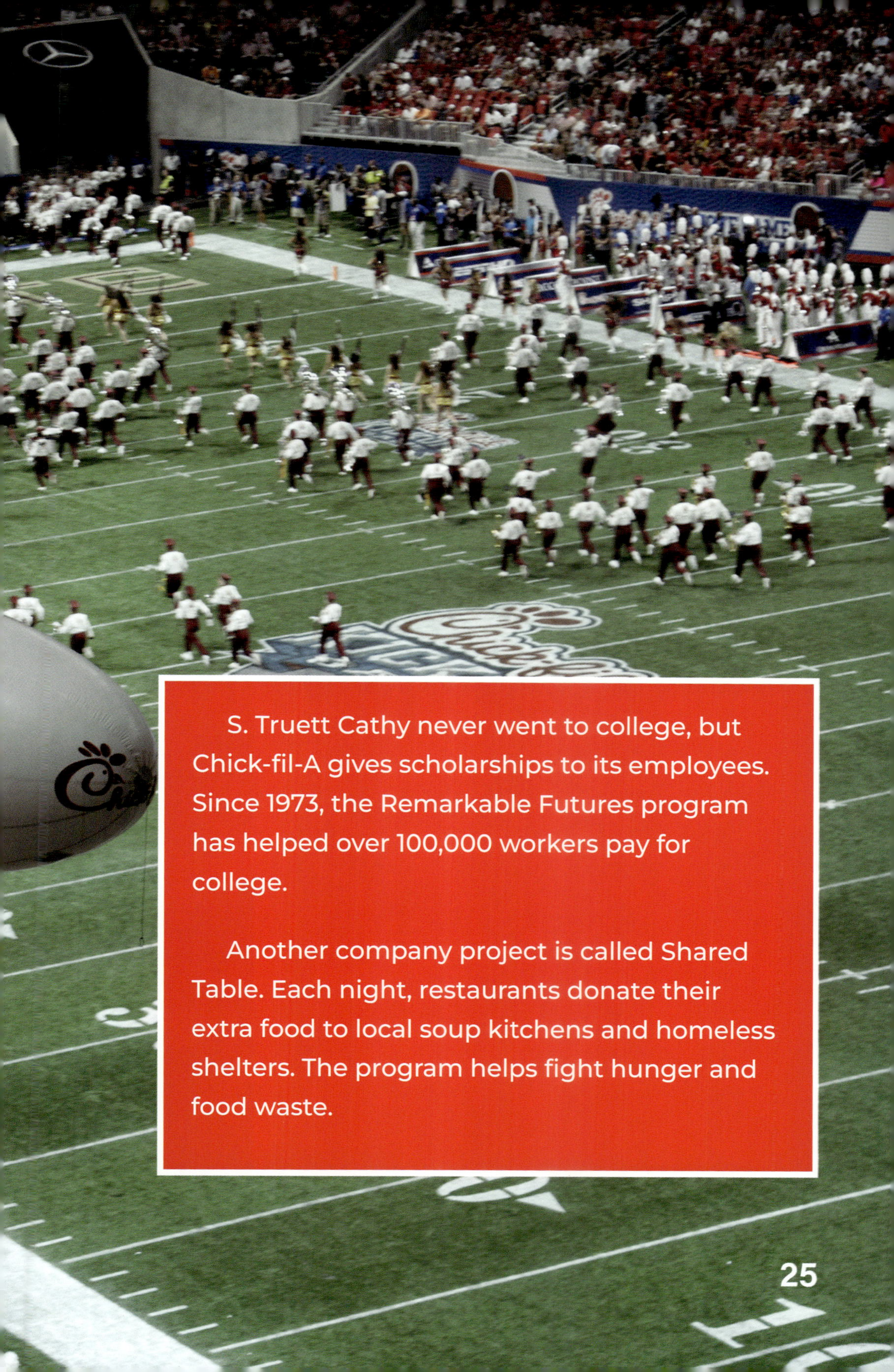

S. Truett Cathy never went to college, but Chick-fil-A gives scholarships to its employees. Since 1973, the Remarkable Futures program has helped over 100,000 workers pay for college.

Another company project is called Shared Table. Each night, restaurants donate their extra food to local soup kitchens and homeless shelters. The program helps fight hunger and food waste.

Chicken isn't the only animal Chick-fil-A is known for. In 1995, two cows appeared on an Atlanta billboard ad for the restaurant. The bovines begged, "EAT MOR CHIKIN."

The cows were on radio and television. They parachuted onto a football field. They were great at getting attention for Chick-fil-A.

Today, the cows can be seen at many locations. After 30 years, they still ask customers to eat less beef and more chicken. Chick-fil-A hopes you'll do just that.

Chick-fil-A
WHEN U EAT CHIKIN,
OWR FUTURE
LOOKZ BRITE
Chick-fil-A
SUITE 408

A CHICK-FIL-A TIME LINE

1946 S. Truett Cathy and his brother Ben open a diner, the Dwarf Grill.

1964 Cathy perfects his chicken sandwich recipe.

1967 The first Chick-fil-A opens in a shopping mall in Atlanta, Georgia.

1984 The company opens its headquarters in Atlanta.

1986 The first stand-alone Chick-fil-A opens in Atlanta.

1995 Cows appear on a Chick-fil-A billboard. They urge people to "EAT MOR CHIKIN." Two black-and-white stars are born.

1996 Chick-fil-A begins to sponsor the Peach Bowl, a college football game played each fall in Atlanta.

2007 The Chick-fil-A cows join the Madison Avenue Walk of Fame, which honors great advertising campaigns.

2014 Founder S. Truett Cathy dies at the age of 93. His family continues to run the company.

2023 The 3,000th Chick-fil-A restaurant opens in Dallas, Texas. The company celebrates by giving 300,000 dollars to two organizations that fight hunger and support education.

GLOSSARY

antibiotic-free (an-ti-bye-AH-tick-free)
not having been given drugs that kill bacteria and that may be harmful to humans

complement (KAHM-pluh-muhnt)
to enhance something by making it whole or making it better than it is on its own

empire (EM-pire)
a large group of businesses controlled by one person, family, or company

founder (FOUN-dur)
the person who starts a company or organization

franchises (fran-CHYE-sis)
individual locations of a chain store or restaurant; legal agreements that let people run businesses that sell products created by a larger company

gathering table (GA-thuh-ring TAY-buhl)
a long table with many places to sit

Great Depression (grayt di-PRESH-uhn)
a period of time from 1929 to 1939 when people around the world did not have much money

marinade (mar-i-NADE)
a sauce in which meat is soaked to tenderize it and enrich its flavor

pressure-cooked (PRESH-ur kukd)
heated in pressurized liquid inside an airtight container to limit boiling, increase cooking temperature, and decrease cooking time

signature (SIG-nuh-chur)
closely associated with someone or something; the most special or well-known menu item at a restaurant

FACT CHECK

1. _________ is important to Chick-fil-A.
   A. Staying open all week B. Religion C. Cooking beef

2. The chicken for Chick-fil-A's signature chicken sandwich is cooked _______.
   A. in each restaurant B. at a factory C. in Atlanta

3. The city most important to Chick-fil-A is __________.
   A. Boston, Massachusetts B. Atlanta, Georgia
   C. New York City, New York

4. The recipe that hasn't changed in 60 years is for Chick-fil-A's _________.
   A. chicken nuggets B. dipping sauce C. chicken sandwich

Answers: 1. B, 2. A, 3. B, 4. C

FURTHER READING

Cohn, Jessica. *On the Job in a Restaurant*. South Egremont, MA: Red Chair Press, 2016.

Hudak, Heather C. *S. Truett Cathy: Chick-fil-A Founder (Food Dudes)*. Minneapolis, MN: ABDO Publishing, 2017.

Kids in the Kitchen. *Chef in Training: 100+ Easy & Yummy Recipes with Cooking Tips*. New York: Kitchen Ink Publishing, 2023.

ON THE INTERNET

Biz Kid$: Young Entrepreneur Profiles
https://bizkids.com/groups/profiles
Learn about young people who have started their own companies.

Chick-fil-A®
https://www.chick-fil-a.com
Learn more about the company and its food.

Food Network: Cooking with Kids
https://www.foodnetwork.com/recipes/packages/recipes-for-kids/cooking-with-kids
Find recipes from the network for fun in the kitchen.

INDEX

ABOUT THE AUTHOR

Laura Purdie Salas is an award-winning author who lives and writes in Minnesota. Her many books include poetry and nonfiction. Laura loves to read, play board games, knit, explore nature, and spend time with her husband and two daughters. She also eats way too much fast food! Her favorite Chick-fil-A items are the bacon breakfast sandwich (with sweet & spicy sriracha sauce!) and their seasonal milkshakes. Visit Laura at laurasalas.com.